8-17-22

Beauty at Night

Also by David J. Rothman

<u>Poetry</u>
Dominion of Shadow, with Allen T. Brown, Gardiner Lithographs, 1996
The Elephant's Chiropractor, Conundrum Press, 1998

<u>Social Science</u>
Hollywood's America, with Stephen Powers and Stanley Rothman, Westview Press, 1996

<u>Editor</u>
The Geography of Hope: Poets of Colorado's Western Slope, Conundrum Press, 1998

Beauty at Night

David J. Rothman
Michael H. Rothman
Cynthia Min

CONUNDRUM

PRESS

Conundrum Press, PO Box 993, Crested Butte, Colorado 81224
Copyright © 2002 by Conundrum Press

All rights reserved. Published 2002.
Printed in the United States of America.

Library of Congress Catalog Number 99-75267

ISBN 0-9657159-5-7

In Memoriam

Cynthia Min (1965-1990)
Michael H. Rothman (1961-1998)

All proceeds from the sale of this book will be donated to the Michael H. Rothman Endowment for Music and the Arts at Crested Butte Academy, a private, independent, secondary boarding and day school in Crested Butte, Colorado.

Table of Contents

Acknowledgments

Lost Creek Letters: "Another Day in Salt Lake"

The Kiss

The Kiss

This kiss
Which is
Between us
Is the trust
That we both give.

We eat to live,
But live to kiss.
Do not eat this,
Do not bite this–
This is a kiss.

Horsetails

O why
Must I
Be a snail?

Look at
Those horses run
In the sun.

Each one has
A flowing tail.

I would like to be running too,
But I cannot.

O why
Must I
Be a snail?

Praise

I scrub my back in a room fifty feet off the ground
As a flock of sparrows whirls around my head, chirping in delight!
It is a bathtub in an apartment with an open window.

My friend whispers to me from Utah,
Telling me about blue sky, white clouds, red rocks, green pines!
It is a telephone.

I zoom across the city in a chair,
The slightest motion of my hands and feet
Deciding my fate, my hours, my journey!
It is a car.

Invisible men and women sing
From the past, from other places, all in a tiny box!
It is a radio.

This comes quietly into your mind.
It is poetry.

Stars

Standing, spinning,
Upward looking,
I saw dropping
Drops of light.

Sitting, sprawling,
Downward falling,
I lay on the grass
And watched the night.

Big Umbrellas

The elephants came walking by,
Holding big umbrellas high.
Their umbrellas kept them dry,
So underneath they did a dance.
The biggest umbrellas in the world
Were held in those elephants' curled
Trunks that day when they walked by
And I got wet, but the elephants
Who danced stayed dry.

It's Broken

Don't be sad.
It can't be that bad.
Please don't cry.
Will it do any good?
Yes, it's broken.
But the best things are not ours.

Look:
Those flags are snapping
In the clear blue sky.
They are holding the day
And the wind and the sun
For a moment and rippling
As it all goes by.

In the Egyptian Garden

Sparrows
Scattered like arrows
From the Pharaoh's
Wheelbarrows.

Old Straw Hat

Do you remember that old straw hat
You gave me when I was young?
I lost that hat long ago.
Sometimes I sit and wonder
What happened to it.

I was walking in the foggy canyon
And suddenly there it was
Just out of reach
And then tumbling down the mountainside.

I've had other straw hats
But that one was the only one
I ever loved
And I lost it
On a gust of wind.

The Icicle Bicycle

The icicle bicycle
Cannot stay cold,
So it never gets
Very old.

The icicle bicycle
Takes you for rides.
When you put on the brake,
It slides.

But your icicle bicycle
Is your own.
There it is, impossible,
Sparkling in the sun.

Leap

Chestnut Tree

Chestnut tree, this is the last time
I will see you preparing to burst
Into pink blossoms. In two months
I will move and next May someone else
Will be drawn to the open window
By the fresh sound of your still-small leaves
Giving the first breeze a voice.
Next time, someone else will notice
The sprigs arching up at the branch ends,
Their buds waiting, waiting.
For what? I don't know,
Because when they open,
Changing the light in the courtyard
As if a cloud had wandered in,
There will still be only a chestnut tree,
Silent, saying nothing, neither happy
Nor unhappy, wise nor foolish,
A place where squirrels run
And birds perch, sometimes to sing.

Old Rose Bushes

They stand on the side of the road
Like grandmothers talking about granddaughters
Too quietly to be heard,
And try to ignore the cold air
Walking in their thorny arms.

One day they will fall
But it won't be this year
Or the next.

Oh, they may look old,
But spring is coming.
I can feel it in my muddy shoes,
It is singing on the other side
Of this hill.

Soon the snow will slouch off
And the fields will whisper
With flowers and grass
As the bears wake up,
Walk out into the sun,
Sniff the crisp air,
Scratch themselves
On the trees' tender bark,
Then sit down
And try to think
What to do next.

Rain

Rain is falling all over the earth.
The people scurry away.
The rain is falling and one man
Puts out his hand. The rain
Is falling, the sky is gray.
The cars go by, the trucks go by
And throw up spray.
The sky is gray,
The rain is falling, plants are drinking
And everything is sinking down
Under the rain.

A man walks through the theater of bowing trees
That stands on the hill. The rain
Is falling all around him, running off his umbrella.
He goes down the path, home
To where the sparrows perch
Under the dripping eaves
Watching the rain that is falling
All over the earth.

O, the sound of the rain
On the ground and the rooftops,
Always the same. . .
O, the sound of the rain.

Blueberries

You know they're ripe when you don't have to tug
Because they easily come off the stem.
They are a sign that summer will end soon.
The stained insides of plastic pails
That come out only once a year
Tell the story of their juices.

The long days have begun to fail
Above town in the unfarmed hills.
The wind which blows late August by
Will turn the leaves as it must
And ripen every farmer's crop in this good year.

Think of all the worlds full of seeds
Setting out today with us
As we go picking sweet blueberries.

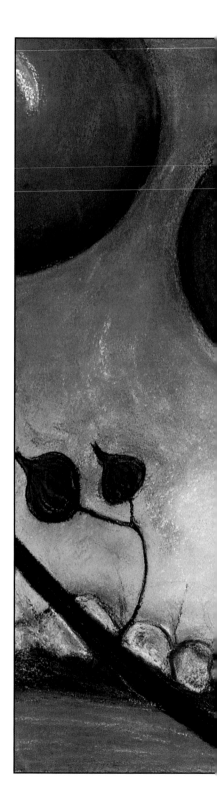

Wind

This is a poem for the wind,
So it should be crystal clear.

What can we say about the wind?
It blows. If it is not blowing
It is not wind. If the leaves outside my window,
Some green, some brown, are not waving,
Whispering and flailing around,
There is no wind. Big wind swirls
Everyone's hair into waves,
Tears kites off the string,
Rips buttons off, dances with newspapers
Spins, rustles, plays autumn out,
Autumn in New York when the haze has blown away.
Sweaters and coats come out of the closet,
And taxi windows roll up. Downtown, please.

The wind is blowing small clouds in lines
Across the Avenues. If you were a cat
Your fur would be thickening and now
You would lie indoors purring on the couch.
The wind in general enjoys making noses
And ears red at this time of year.

The autumn wind has arrived.
It is the wind of sailboats
That tilt in the sparkling harbor.
It is riffling the banners.
It is the breath of the world.

Fire

The moon is not
Made out of fire.
Your eyes are not
Made out of fire
Except when you don't get
Something you want.

What happens when the moon
Does not get what she wants,
The long thin clouds racing
And heavy tides crashing
To do her work?
She does not get angry
And rain fire on us
As that is not her idea
Of getting things done.
She leaves that to the sun.

Her fires are colder.
They smolder
On the dark side of the moon
In the old volcanoes
Where eclipses come from.

Man and Tree

—For Monica

1.

The leaves hang on the tree
In bunched ovals of limp, moist brown.

It's not enough for me,
I say, you're free
Now, it's time to fall down.

The leaves hang on the tree.

It doesn't matter to me,
I say, how much you clown—
It's not enough for me
Just to know your summer memory
Is a lie—I want to watch you fall.

                              I frown.

The leaves hang on the tree.

It's winter, I say, the sky is icy.
Give up. You make a poor crown.
It's not enough for me
If I can't see the black branches clearly—
The end of every seed that's sown—
It's not enough for me.

The leaves hang on the tree.

2.

Oh little man
Do not be so sad
Just because I
Am the last tree on the block
With a few yellow leaves
And when the wind blows I laugh
At all my companions who are so stiff,
Dark, and dreary in their bare state.
I don't do it to torture your memory.
Just think how pleasant it will be
When the birds come back, as they will,
And build nests in my hands.
I'll smile and sway like a fool
And you will too.

This is a feeling I never abandon,
As spring is inevitable
And has nothing to do with my own hopes.

You look warm enough anyway,
All bundled up like that.
Things could be worse.
You might have to stand out here like me
And sleep alone one January.

I can see I haven't convinced you.
I hope someone else can speak
For me, someone who loves you
And will leave a note on your desk
That explains all this, since you
Have clearly misunderstood
Everything.

Leap

A tiger jumps
From all the high apartments,
Lands gracefully and then climbs
Back up to jump again.

He never bothers the residents,
But just pads noiselessly in and leaps
With a tiger smile.

When he noses into my room
I try to tell him my name,
But he doesn't even flick a whisker.
He is not interested in me.

It is like a birthday,
The sweet surprise
As the tiger lopes past and leaps.

March in Massachusetts

Come back. Don't ramble around
In the south any more,
Massaging Patagonia.

Come here. Come out.
Don't go away again
Leaving this snow on the ground,
This ice on the pond.

Push into the sky
As if you knew
You were always right.
Drive a little warmth
Through the air.

Come back.
Sing to the grass.
Make it grow like hair.
Tell us now, we want to hear
About black mud, tight buds
And new bark growing.

The Answer

Another Day in Salt Lake

My cat is sad. He is hiding under a blanket, making sounds like a confused bird. Only his tail is showing. Outside the window the Piccardy apartments are slowly being devoured by fog.

Everything only turns grayer.

Suddenly the cat charges around the apartment three times with his ears back, turns into a ball of fire and flies out the window. The plants applaud and the Piccardy begins to reappear as the cat does acrobatics high above the pedestrians, who are bored as usual and don't even think about looking up, who believe that flying cats do not exist.

I lean out the window yelling at the cat: "What am I going to do with all this cat food?" Returning, however, seems to be beyond his capacity. He is pursued over the landscape by a flock of pigeons which had only flown in circles before this.

Several days later I see him walking straight down the side of the building. Fat and purring he comes to my arms, but refuses to say where he has been.

The Kite

I sat down to think of you
But my thoughts escaped me
Like a kite snapping freely
At the end of a long string.
The string ends in a stick
Where more of it is wrapped.
A boy and girl take turns holding the stick
In the crisp, autumn afternoon.
Who are they?
They live outside of town.

Now they are running through a field,
Trailing me behind. Now they've stopped
And are watching me,
Shielding their eyes with their hands.

They are both
Alone in their thoughts.

The wind is rushing around me.
The world is so small down there.
I am sending this to you.

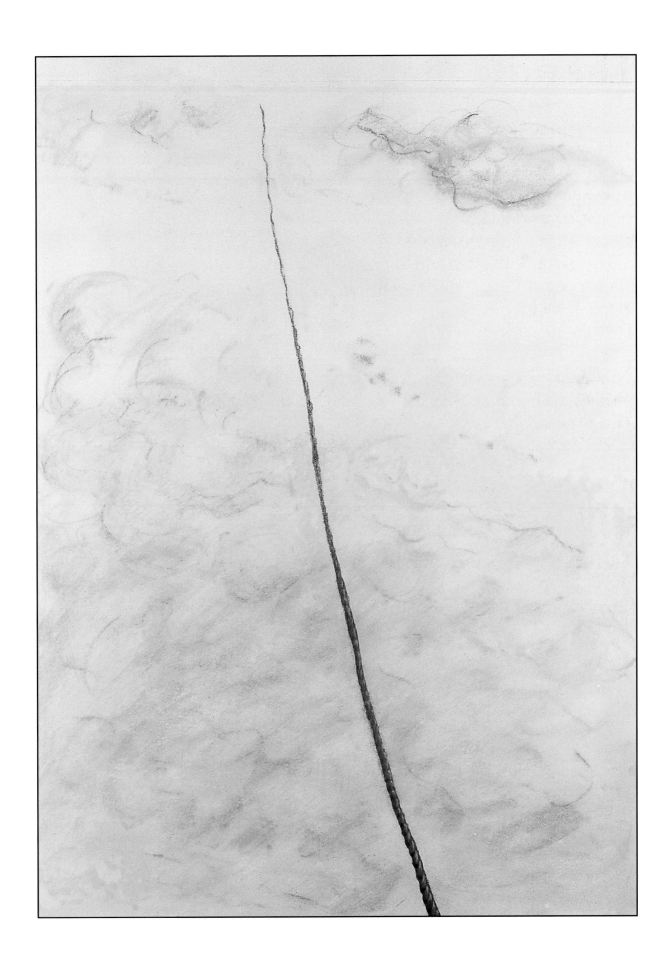

Stunned Finch

The finch was fine. I had been holding it,
Then it was flying back and forth in the rafters
Of the barn, then out the door. I didn't see
It stun itself on a beam or wall, then fall.
I found it after that, mysterious,
A sleeping yellow thumb with folded wings,
Eyes closed, heart quick, small feathers on small chest
Senselessly ruffling in the breezes crossing
The hay-covered floor.
                                    It woke up with a start
Upon my clumsy palm, blinked twice, and then
Decided to go, first up into the rafters,
Then out the door and up into the sky.

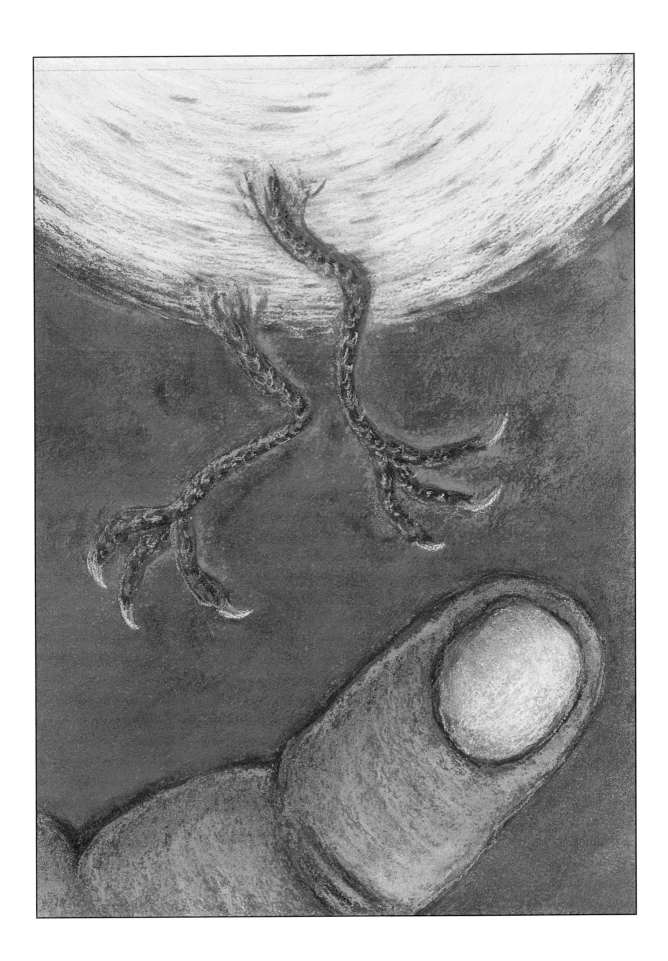

The Answer

Hello. You have reached the poem
Of David J. Rothman. I am not here
Just now. I am someplace else.
Maybe I am looking
At something you cannot see:
The old stone fence where squirrels walk.
Or eating a sandwich, probably corned beef,
My favorite, on rye, with mustard and sauerkraut.
Maybe I am doing
Nothing at all just now.

But one thing is clear:
I am not here.

To be honest, I never was.
These words were never my home.
They came first
And only asked me to appear afterwards,
The way the sun waits for the earth to rise,
The way we must have hours
Before we can make watches.

If you would like to leave a message
You are out of luck,
Because the I who was never here
Is never coming back.
Instead, however, you might pick up a pen.
Do not write me a letter.
I am out of town, on the lam,
Snipping roses in Normandy,
Sleeping in Dublin, dining in Shanghai,
Living on a river in the moon.
Besides, my mouth is full of flowers.
I would probably never get back to you.

Instead, try to find a word,
A word that does something,
Something strange and unimaginable,
As unimaginable as I am,
A word that does something
Like rhyme with "window,"
Or leave a taste in someone else's ear.

Noise

Do you like noise? Come over to my place.
Behind my apartment four guys
Who never stop yelling and yammering
Are building an addition to the ground floor.
Today they're jackhammering
The hole for a new door.
The leader is trying to teach
The young guy with the jackhammer.
Together they will soon reach
A level of noise that could strangle summer.
No! he howls, Don't close your eyes!
No! Not straight! At an angle!
At an angle! Like this! Understand?

Somebody I don't know lives
On the other side of my wall.
This month, every night, she gives
Her nights to home repair.
Just as I start to fall
Asleep, she starts to scrape.
There's no escape.
She's always there.
I am beginning to think that
She's actually a giant rat.

Add to this the hum and whir of appliances,
The roar of cars, buses, fire engines, ambulances,
Police sirens, airplanes, subways, helicopters,
Televisions, radios, and July fireworks,
And it begins to seem as if noise
Is what the city most enjoys.
It's too loud here to get a poem done.
I don't know how I wrote this one.

The Interruption

. . . just then we saw a man
Slowly mopping his way down the hall,
Head lowered like a bull.
He would not stop mopping
The linoleum floor. We sang reason
After reason at him, we pleaded
Like a springtime snowpatch for more time.
But he backed us towards the wall
Until we had to elbow and kick
Our way past plaster and brick
And trust our luck to a walk on air.
We hurried away, looking back
Over our shoulders. Still he followed us,
Like a rowing angel, over the city.
We hid in the clouds.
Ah, here we can talk.

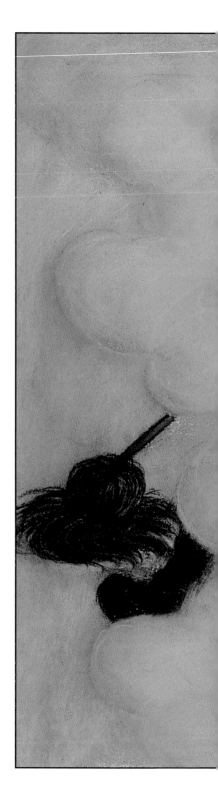

The Wall

I would describe the wall,
But I can't decide which matters more,
The rocks or the cracks.

The rocks are bigger, but facts
Are facts, and we would never see them
Standing as wall
If it weren't for the cemented cracks
That won't let them fall.

Those cracks write their own life.
They feather out in a leaping way.
But if you look at them all day
You will forget what it is
They are supposed to hold together:
The rocks.

So how can you tell the rocks
From the cracks? Maybe it's not a question
Worth worrying about,
One we could ever figure out.
And anyway there are other things to see.
Most of the stonecutters have left
Because the wall is almost done.
Only one old man remains,
Plinking away at the reddish stone
And the summer sun
Is finally setting
Behind the hills.

I Do Not Understand

I have woken up in the morning again and again,
Roared sometimes, yawned on others,
Grown a beard and spoken in a deep voice,
Filled my ears with wax
And stared at the moon as it sailed by
And still I do not understand.
I do not understand why you are leaving,
Like a cloud, or the sun
At the end of the day.

Will you forgive me
For failing as a magician?
Will we all become coals
That glow with secrets of love?

Sleep, and I will close this book,
I will run my fingers through your hair
Before turning out the light.
Then, with your breathing, explain to me
Where you are going, and why.

Washing My Feet

I stand in the shower,
Clear water streams around me,
The sun shines through a window,
I wash the spaces between my toes.
I wash away the dirt
That has grown there as I
Went walking over the earth
Like a question mark.
To do this I raise one foot
And run soapy fingers
Around and across and through
Wherever I can.
Then I do the other one
The same way.
Standing like a stork is slippery
But necessary in the shower,
To wash my dirty feet.
The water dances on my skin.
I step out, rub myself dry,
And once again the earth whispers
"Begin."

Beauty at Night

Michael H. Rothman

Works of art speak for themselves. The temperament and personality of artists, and the historical context in which they work, although essential to a complete understanding of their art, cannot be the central focus of a meaningful analysis of a piece of work. Such an approach can easily degenerate into indulgent gossip that tends to devalue the work in favor of a cult of personality.

Used properly, however, these factors can set the stage for a discussion of specific works of art, and in the case of a comparison of Magritte's *Empire of Lights* and Van Gogh's *Starry Night*, observations on the personalities of these two painters provide valuable insights into how they perceive and represent beauty in a nighttime landscape.

One would be hard pressed to find two more diverse artistic temperaments than those of Van Gogh and Magritte. Van Gogh was a violently tormented misfit who never came to terms with society or accepted himself. Magritte was a calm, contented fellow, who blended easily with the crowd and led a singularly uneventful and well-adjusted personal life.

Starry Night, Vincent Van Gogh

Although *Starry Night* is a more quintessential example of Van Gogh's work than *Empire of Lights* is of Magritte's, these personality traits are nonetheless singularly evident.

Starry Night pulsates violently. The artist's palette covers the entire spectrum of color. Van Gogh weaves opposite colors in and out of immediate proximity to each other, breaking down the distinction between elements. Sky and land battle and penetrate each other. The painting presents an unsettling vision of nature in constant flux and at odds with itself, and, by implication, at odds with the artist.

Van Gogh's vivid, assertive brushwork echoes and reinforces this feeling, questioning the boundaries of objects and their environment. The result is a thrilling, uncertain, and vaguely disquieting beauty that seems almost dangerous in its intensity. The viewer is forced to gaze with apprehensive wonder, and attempt to evaluate his or her own relationship with nature and beauty, for who could sleep on a night like this? Certainly not Vincent. Objects are not really objects here, they lack solidity and integrity, there is no specific light source to

Empire of Lights, René Magritte   ©1999 C. Herscovici, Brussels Artists Rights Society (ARS), New York

define them in a space. Even space is not really itself, for it lacks any feeling of emptiness. The bright opposing colors in squiggling spirals destroy the conventional perspective on reality. Paradoxically, these threatening ideas which are central to Van Gogh's triumphantly successful vision of beauty seem to be lost on the recent generation of troubled adolescents who have placed reproductions of *Starry Night* firmly in the dorm room top ten. They simply and unconsciously respond. They do not realize that it was Van Gogh's very fear of emptiness that drove him to fill his canvas with so much of the passionate color they see simply as "beauty."

Empire of Lights sits still in subtle, serene elegance, a triumph of understatement. The boundaries of objects and their placement in space are rock solid. A limited palette of subdued yet pure colors applied with intelligence and care adds to a feeling of peace. The artist and viewer can breathe easily tonight, secure in a well-ordered world where everything is as it should be. A feeling of silence pervades the land and sky in a comforting and extremely inhabitable world. Once this feeling has been sufficiently absorbed, however, an inevitable double take occurs, for Magritte is not without his own sense of the wonder and mystery of the night, and this is the common ground of these two paintings. What is the source of this mystery? Perhaps it lies in the eerie brightness of the sky, which one would think, after looking at the darkness on the ground, would be darker, even starry. Magritte seems to be saying that the unseen force that creates such a perfectly ordered world can light up a nighttime sky without boldly announcing itself to our earthbound lives.

In *Starry Night*, every element possesses its own luminosity. The play between well-defined sources of light and darkness in *Empire of Lights* provides a cornerstone for this sense of mystery in quite the opposite way. In *Starry Night*, everything is said but nothing is known. In *Empire of Lights*, everything is known but nothing is said.

Both the violence and the serenity of the night are mysterious and beautiful. The approach and artistic temperament of these two artists are ideally suited for the expression of these opposing, yet complementary views.

New York City
December 12, 1986

50

Empire of Lights, René Magritte

51

Afterword

David J. Rothman

This book is dedicated with great love to the memory of my younger brother, Michael Hillel Rothman, and his lover, Cynthia Min, who collaborated on all the artwork. They were talented, vivacious people, both of whom died of drug overdoses.

Cindi died in 1990 at the age of 25, of an overdose of "ice," a smokeable synthetic methamphetamine, when she and Michael were living in Taipei, Taiwan, making a living of sorts as street musicians and small-time drug dealers. After lighting up, she announced she was going to take a bath. Michael found her in the tub, where she had died of a ruptured aorta.

Michael was secretive about his personal life, and so I only met Cindi once, over the long weekend of my father's sixtieth birthday in August, 1987. I am not even sure if she preferred "Cynthia" or "Cindi" as her name, and I am not positive about her age when she died. I don't think anyone in my family other than Michael ever met anyone in hers, although I believe she was raised in Hawaii. I do know that she and Michael lived together on and off for at least two or three years, mostly in Asia, after having graduated together from the San Francisco Art Institute in the mid 1980s. I do know that Michael loved her deeply, and I could see why. She was a talented, charming, beautiful woman.

Cindi was reserved when I met her, but she was visiting her lover's family and staying in their home for the first time, and Michael was fighting with our parents over the usual things: money, typically chaotic travel plans, the larger issue of what he was going to do with his life, all of it riding the current of the drug abuse, which they didn't understand. Over the years, pieces of Cindi's artwork began to appear in our home. When I would visit there would be a drawing in a desk drawer, or a painted bluejean jacket hanging in a closet. She was a better draughtsman than Michael, and her work had a whimsical quality. Although Michael was a good artist, I don't think he could have executed the drawings for this book with the same clarity on his own. I see her hand in most, if not all, of the originals, in the careful and gentle choice of color and the thoughtful detail. I'm not sure, but I expect that Michael conceptualized most of the pieces and roughed them out, and then he and Cindi worked together to finish them. Without her involvement they would not be as strong, and might not even exist, as I think she was the more disciplined about getting things done.

For years she and Michael led a ragged life of the demi-monde, traipsing from one far eastern city to another, earning a living by "busking" (playing street music), getting money from our parents (and perhaps hers), and occasionally dealing drugs (including narcotics). I know that she had at least one tubular pregnancy which nearly killed her, in part because she and Michael avoided western medicine. I wish I had known her better, but I am grateful for the excellent work she did on this book. Her death was a waste.

When Cindi died, Michael was devastated, but denied for months that her death had anything to do with drug use. I talked with him on the phone in Asia for hours over a period of weeks and finally convinced him to enroll in a drug treatment program at McLean Hospital near Boston. He lasted for a while, then got caught smoking pot and was told to leave. He did so—one of the moments when I felt I was helplessly watching him let his life run through his fingers. In all the time he was a drug abuser I rarely if ever heard him say that he really wanted to quit, or that his drug use was dangerous and destructive, even though Cindi was not the only person in his life who died of an overdose. He had made his choice.

Michael was my only sibling. He was born on August 1, 1961, two years, two months, and 19 days after me, unfortunately too close given our family and our personalities. He died just after he turned 37, on August 15, 1998, in Seoul, South Korea, of what was probably an accidental overdose of a codeine-based prescription drug he was taking for depression. At the time of his death he was teaching English as a second language in a school set up specifically for that purpose, but he had lost his job, as he had lost the one before that, and was staying in a hotel. He had started to have what were probably psychotic breaks, during which he became incoherent, delusional, and confused, and his employers would simply let him go. In the early stages of these episodes, he would become manic and call my parents or me from Asia in the middle of the night and rant about whatever was on his mind. Sometimes it was to talk about a book he'd read; other times it was more unhinged, like the time he called in the early hours of the morning to accuse me of having always been jealous of the size of his penis. It's hard to say if these monologues which began in the last few years of his life were the product of excessive narcotics and psychotropic drug use for decades, or that his drug use had been a way to self-medicate an underlying bipolar or other condition. Probably both.

I know where I was when my brother was born, though I don't remember it. I also know where I was when Michael died. I was 39 years, three months, and three days old, camping on a field of wildflowers under a canopy of stars with my wife, Emily, and our four-year-old son, Jacob. We were at Paradise Divide, a few miles to the northwest of Crested Butte, Colorado, where we still live.

Paradise Divide sits at 11,200 feet, beneath mountains that climb thousands of feet higher. At that time of year, near the end of its brief summer, it looks like the world made new every morning. The Maroon Bells loom in the distance, but the terrain around the Divide is relatively gentle, pastures of wildflowers and scree flowing off in every direction. I sat out that night before going to sleep, thinking under a starry sky about Michael, whom I knew was suffering again, and wondering if he would survive. Even as I wondered, my career as a brother ended. I can never be a brother again.

Most people are unfamiliar with how addiction works on a daily basis, and see only confusion, pain, and manipulation. In Michael's case, as for so many others, his problems as an addict were so overwhelming that many who knew him—especially his immediate family—had trouble looking past his self-destructive behavior and the pain it regularly brought to him and to others. For many, he became his problem. But while drugs did frequently dominate his life, there was certainly more to the man than that. As his contemporary and brother, I came to see, and continued to love, a charming, intelligent, funny, creative man with a terrible disease. Learning how to separate the two was a long process, including a year spent teaching English at DaySpring, a drug rehabilitation center for adolescents in Salt Lake City. It was only after working in a team with the counselors there that I came to understand what it would mean to hold my brother fully accountable for his own actions, and how to avoid the many traps he regularly set to ensnare me as a supporter of his illness. For as anyone who has ever been involved with addicts eventually learns, they will do anything to get others—family members, friends, lovers, colleagues, and anyone else in the neighborhood—to enable them to avoid responsibility for their own self-destructive actions. Lies, threats, denials, obfuscations: my brother knew all the tricks, and in the middle of an addictive compulsion, would do anything he could to shift responsibility away from himself and on to others. Recognizing that this behavior was only one part of a complex person was the only way to continue to love him, although it often led to painful confrontations, such as when I refused to agree to remain silent when I knew he was lying to our parents about how he was spending the money they gave him.

My brother's problems were grave. In the end, they killed him. But there were also good times. Among other things, we shared a certain sense of humor like a game of catch. On the best days, we could find a language that I know I cannot ever share with anyone ever again for the rest of my life:

> "*Wine Spectator*. Dumb name." "Right. A magazine for people who look at wine." "What could they have done? *Wine Drinker*?" "I see your point. Troubling connotations there. Why not just embrace them?" "*Drinker's Monthly*?" "*Package Store*." "*Wino!*" "*Guzzler*". . .

Exit to a long list of potential articles, features, and reviews. At least he could laugh about it.

Michael was also a good junior athlete who squandered his ability the way he squandered everything else. One time we were swimming together across a small lake in the Berkshire Hills of Massachusetts, where we grew up. We had set out from a public beach, and crossed the line closing in the small patrolled area. A lifeguard hastily rowed up and informed us that state law required that we swim within the ropes, to which Michael, treading water, replied, "What about if we swim with our own ropes?"

Michael was a talented musician who never fully developed his talents. Our mother has perfect pitch, and Michael's relative pitch was accurate to the quaver. He studied classical cello when young, and then became a folk, rock, and jazz guitarist, spending several years working part-time in nightclubs across Asia. He was also a good artist, and while earning his undergraduate degree from the Art Institute he also ran a small film festival. By the time he was fifteen he was producing canvases that still compel twenty-five years later. We would spend hours, late into the night, arguing about Italian cinema, about jazz, about surrealism. The difference was that, when it came to art, Michael could draw what he was describing, and I could not. I would counter with a sonnet. He would parry with a guitar lick. I would thrust with a piano fingering. For the last several years of his life he taught English in several Asian countries (something I had also done in the People's Republic of China), and I have to believe that he was a good teacher as well. He was too bright, articulate, and charming not to be. Since his death, several of his friends have contacted my family and said that Michael's passion for art, sense of humor, exuberance, and loyalty changed their lives.

We also argued about drugs as his problems worsened, although it wasn't until I spent that year as a teacher at DaySpring that I began to see that everything that he did when it came to drug use could have served as a series of illustrations in a twelve-step textbook. He was an addict. In his fear and pain, he compulsively confused intoxication with happiness. Choice, predisposition, or self-medication, the need to be high dominated his life, and he defended that need the way the Russians defended Stalingrad. When I finally told him, in our mid-twenties, that I wouldn't support this behavior any more, either by act or silence, he flew into a rage. If I told our parents he was using the money they gave him to buy drugs, he was going to stop talking to me. If I refused to allow him to stay with me if he were using drugs, he would never stay with me again even if he were clean. He tried to convince me that his drug use (including regular narcotics use) was less dangerous than drinking, that his relationship with our parents was none of my business, that he had it all under control. "Look, I'm your only brother and when our parents are gone I'll be the only family you've got, so you better treat me better if you want to see me after they die." Pretty standard stuff from a bright doper, all of which made good glib sense, except that I had finally accepted I was dealing with someone who once gave himself an abscess by mainlining ground-up Ritalin through a Bic pen.

I made it clear I wouldn't move. He did enter rehab twice and failed (once at McClean, once at the Meadows, a facility in Arizona). Not only Cindi, but other people in his vicinity dropped dead with distressing frequency, including friends and lovers; people would call my parents threatening to kill him; he did over a year in a Thailand prison for credit card fraud, all the result of drugs. When he got out, he convinced my parents to give him several thousand dollars, disappeared into the slums of Manila for a few weeks where he spent it all in whorehouses, then called and asked for more. We had a bit of a family fight about that one (my position being that you don't give money to a junkie), but the interesting thing was that in his conversations with me, as opposed to with my parents, he let me know what he had actually done, even though he knew I wouldn't keep it a secret for him. He had an unusual gift for strewing chaos among those who loved him, and could do it like a puppeteer from thousands of miles away. Yet despite the fact that Michael's wild life and addiction gave him less and less happiness as he grew older, he was never able even to commit to quitting, much less to quit. He simply had too much invested in being an outlaw.

At one point about fifteen years ago I warned my parents that one day we were probably going to get a phone call which would begin, "I am calling from the American Embassy in (pick some Asian state). I am sorry to inform you that. . ." Still, as I now know, nothing can prepare you for that call.

This book is one of the tangible remaining pieces of our brotherhood, and therefore precious. And its genesis has little to do with drug addiction, but much with art. These poems and paintings didn't emerge from pathology, but from careful thought, study, and love. What they mostly reflect are some ideas about poetry and art which Michael and I (and I think Cindi) shared. For me, and for Michael, they were the product of a conscious decision to go in a certain direction with our creative work.

When I graduated from college in 1982, I had the good luck to land a job for the summer working as a gardener at Les Bois de Moutiers, a landscape and formal garden in Normandy near the village of Varengeville-sur-Mer, about ten kilometers down the Channel coast from Dieppe. The job was ideal for a young American eager to see Europe. I would be on my own, earning my keep, and learning something about gardening.

Les Bois des Moutiers is a charmed place. The 60-hectare landscape garden is one of the few of its kind in France. The Normandy coast is an ideal place to grow an astonishing variety of plants, and the garden includes everything from roses to rhododendrons the size of houses to redwood trees. It is laced with paths and is a place of solace. It also has an astonishingly rich cultural history, far too long and complex to recount here. The currents of fin de siécle French cultural life swirled around it. The architect who designed the house in 1900 was Edward Lutyens and the owners, the Mallet family, moved in circles which included the theosophists, Gide, Cocteau, Krisnamurti and other figures of comparable stature.

Into all of this I stepped knowing nothing. I had been hired in a rather confused process by a friend of a friend of the owner, Robert Mallet, and arrived not knowing quite what to expect. I spent the summer learning the basics of gardening, working with the hired help. I dug out the broken septic tank; I weeded an entire garden of rat grass, a recalcitrant weed; I would spend an entire morning snipping wilted roses; I watered the potted plants and mowed the great lawn; I was taught how to brain moles with a shovel.

All summer I lived in a little house near one edge of the upper, formal gardens, far enough from the big house to feel quite alone. It had a small kitchen, bathroom, and tiny bedroom, and was a damp, stucco place. I spent my days gardening, then windsurfing with the younger Mallet generation and their friends in the late afternoons at one of the nearby beaches. Weekends I would jump a train to Paris and wander from museum to museum, living on coffee, cheap wine, and croissants.

In Varengeville there were small shops where I could buy local bread, cheese, and wine for my cupboard, although I took most of my meals with the family in the kitchen. After dinner I would stroll back to my little house, as mist and fog drifted up from the Channel and across the garden in the long Normandy dusk, the distant sound of foghorns rising and ebbing with it. And with a glass of wine and some fresh local chevre, I would sit and try to write poems.

That is where this book began. Of course I continued to write the complex, elusive, self-conscious, fractured, post-modernist lyrics which grew out of my undergraduate years. But living and working in that garden, surrounded by so much which seemed to communicate so calmly, so clearly, and so unabashedly beautifully, something else began to happen, and one day I resolved to try to write a group of poems which would be clearer, less convoluted, more direct. I felt a desperate need to make something in a language which would be accessible and meaningful to others. Strange, but in one of the places linked to Symbolism I was inspired to go in the opposite direction.

I started the poems in *Beauty at Night* as exercises, not thinking of making them into a book. They were meant to make me more verbally honest, to help me move away from the splintered lyric of subjective perception, of dark, impossible epistemological riddles, which seemed so exhausted and exhausting. I wanted to write poems which would give some pleasure and be understood. I wanted to write poems that had nothing to do with me, but which would convey wonder. I wanted to make a small garden of poems, a place to walk and be at peace.

A year or two later, when I showed some of them to Jeanne Heifetz, a friend back in America, she said that they were obviously children's poems, something that had never occurred to me. But once she suggested it, I decided to see if I could write enough of them to make a manuscript.

One night in the late 1980s I showed them to Michael in the course of a long conversation about art and poetry. While neither of us objected to abstraction per se, we both felt that in our respective arts there was a stultifying anti-representational orthodoxy. In poetry, academic free verse still reigned in the schools; my objection to this was partly formal, but ultimately generic and imaginative. In everything I read, it seemed, poets were expected to be both sincere and obscure. What a dull curse. Novelists, dramatists, film makers, they were expected to create dynamic fictions, free to lie, but the voice of poetry was supposed to be authentic and personal at all times, whether discussing ideas or experiences, all of it couched in tepid, unrhymed, unmetered verse whose lineation broke against syntax. As if that stranger, our reader, cares, or should care, about our lives. Some writers sought to break out of this with politics, but usually became merely strident. I felt that most of the poetry I was encountering and which was earning praise was written for a coterie of narcissists. It's important to remember that at that time, although Richard Wilbur, Anthony Hecht and a few others were continuing to write metrically, they were considered hopeless reactionaries by the generation which had succeeded them, and it was almost impossible to place a single rhymed couplet in an American poetry journal. To present a poem which told a story in a poetry workshop would be to risk derogatory comparisons with the Roman Empire. No one seemed willing to believe that one could conceivably enjoy both free verse and metrical forms, confessions and fictions, a mix of truth and lies.

Michael responded that he felt the same way about the contemporary art scene, that although he enjoyed abstraction he thought that representational painting was a perfectly legitimate and serious form. He said how tired he was of having to back up paintings with concepts, as if every canvas required a manifesto because otherwise it was incomprehensible. He said that he, too, wanted to make some paintings and drawings which were good without being difficult, which were not enmeshed in obscure forests of symbol, which did not muddy the paint to make it look deep, which didn't require a treatise to justify them as meaningful, when all they needed to be was beautiful, and, God forbid, perhaps even fun.

That's how we decided to make this book. For two young artists (and then three with the addition of Cindi) it was a joyous opportunity to make something in which we could believe—a disciplined, serious art which was representational and accessible, playful yet committed, built on a sound, diverse technique. In short, we did our best to make a book which was based on a common language, in the belief that that language would appeal to others.

When I first saw Michael and Cindi's drawings, I was elated. They had done exactly what they had said they were going to do. Every drawing was not just an illustration, but a companion. Each one playfully leaves things out, referring to things larger and beyond itself, either within the poem or beyond it. The drawing of the kite shows only the string; the drawing of the tiger shows only the tail; the Chinese hat has turned into a bird's nest. The framing of the drawings suggests an imaginative and real world thriving beyond and outside itself. They gave and still give me delight, because they are evidence that the poems had leapt across to other people, who then created something new in return. In fact, I think many of the illustrations are better than the poems.

The deeper joy came because it was my own troubled brother who had created these drawings. We had met and collaborated on a wide imaginative field. We had made something lasting and good together, rooted in clear thinking and meaningful purpose.

Michael taught me about film, about folk music, and about painting. Some of the short pieces of his writing about art which survive are luminous. The essay on Van Gogh and Magritte which I have reprinted here, and whose title provides the title of this book, is a piece he wrote as an undergraduate. It shows how well he understood the deep emotional realities of painting. The fact that, in our troubled relationship, we were able to come together to make this book is a moment of grace for which I am profoundly grateful.

In addition to teaching me about his art, Michael taught me, despite himself, the difficult skills of dealing with an addict. More importantly, he taught me how to be a brother, an understanding I now carry as both burden and blessing. Had he lived and overcome his problems, he would have made a more significant contribution to the world. The book in your hands is one of the few shining moments of an unhappy and unfulfilled life and brotherhood, and yet it stands as a testimony to the redeeming power of creative work and love. Despite its troubled genesis, I hope it gives you the joy all of its authors wished to convey.

Crested Butte, Colorado
Spring, 2002

62

Michael and David Rothman

September 8, 1991

Edwin Gaynor